Crater Lake National Park

GUIDE BOOK

The Ultimate Crater Lake Handbook: Insider Edition for a Journey Beyond the Ordinary!

JULIE MOORE

Copyright © by JULIE MOORE. All rights reserved

Before this document is duplicated or reproduced in any manner, the publisher's consent must be gained.

Therefore, the contents within can neither be stored electronically,

Transferred, nor kept in a database. Neither in part

Nor in full can the document be copied, scanned, faxed, or retained without approval from the publisher or creator.

TABLE OF CONTENT

CHAPTER 1: INTRODUCTION

    Welcome to Crater Lake National Park

    Unveiling the Cascade Jewel:

    A Glance at History:

    Park essentials:

CHAPYER 2: Top Attractions

    Crater Lake, The Crown Jewel:

    Beyond the Crown Jewel

    Unveil the Magic

CHAPTER 3: Wildlife Viewing

Diverse BirdLife

Loons, the haunting melody of the deep.

Encounters in the Wild

Marmots and Pika: Playful Master of the Alpine

CHAPTER 4: Hiking and Trekking Trails

Unveiling Crater Lake's Majesty: Hiking Trails for Everyone

Garfield Peak Trail

The Echo Canyon Trail

Pacific Crest Trail

CHAPTER 5: Photography Opportunities

Unveiling the Soul of Crater Lake

Dawn's Fiery Embrace, Twilight's Farewell Kiss

Nature's Kaleidoscope

Creatures of the Night

Starry Spectacle

CHAPTER 6: Adventure Sports

Kayaking and Stand-Up Paddle boarding

Winter Wonderland

CHAPTER: 7 Educational Programs

Ranger-Led Talks and Walks

Junior Ranger Activities

Crater Lake Discovery

More than just programs:

CHAPTER: 8 My Suggested Additions

Geology and Volcanology Tours

Cultural and Tribal History Programs

Art and Photography Workshops

CHAPTER 9: Activities for Every Traveler

For nature enthusiasts

For the Determined Hiker

For the Thrill Seeking Adventurer

For the history buff

For Relaxation and Rejuvenation

For families

CHAPTER 10: Itineraries for Different Visits

1-Day Exploration

Weekend Getaway

CHAPTER 11: Essential Information

Lodging & Dining

In-park Options:

Nearby Options

Budget-conscious choices:

Camping and backpacking

Obtaining Permits and Regulations:

Responsible practices

Additional considerations:

Transportation

Visitor Centers & Park Headquarters

CHAPTER 12: Beyond the Park

Exploring Nearby Towns and Attractions

Day Trips to Bend, Oregon

Sustainable travel practices

Appendix

CHAPTER 1: INTRODUCTION

Welcome to Crater Lake National Park

Hello, nature lovers, adventure seekers, and fellow wander lusters! Consider this your official invitation to Crater Lake National Park, a site that will leave you breathless, dumbfounded, and most likely racing for your camera at every turn. I'm not just another visitor reciting information from a leaflet; I've hiked these volcanic slopes, inhaled the fresh mountain air, and peered into the fascinating depths of Crater Lake enough times to feel like a local. So consider me your unofficial guide, ready to reveal the secrets of this breathtaking treasure.

Unveiling the Cascade Jewel:

Consider this: a crystal-clear lake so vibrantly blue that it appears to glow from within, surrounded by a volcano crater formed ages ago. Towering evergreens frame the picture, their emerald cloak standing out against the austere grey cliffs that rise magnificently. This isn't a postcard, folks; it's Crater Lake, a living monument to the Earth's fiery past and a haven for nature enthusiasts like us.

A Glance at History:

Millions of years ago, Mount Mazama, a powerful volcano, loomed tall. The summit then fell in a spectacular eruption that shook the ground to its very foundations, leaving behind a massive crater. Nature gradually filled the crater with snowmelt, transforming it into the deepest lake in the United States. For millennia, this holy site whispered stories to Native American tribes, and in 1902, Crater Lake National Park was established to preserve its grandeur for future generations.

Park essentials:

Ready to start your own Crater Lake adventure? Let us get you prepared. This park is open year-round, but each season creates a unique masterpiece. Summer blooms with wildflowers in a blaze of color, while winter turns the slopes into a snowy paradise ideal for snowshoeing or cross-country skiing. Spring delivers soothing streams and rich vegetation, while October paints the mountains in flaming colors that will leave you stunned. Choose your season, pack your bags (layers are essential!) and remember that accessibility is a primary focus here. Paved pathways, marked overlooks, and visitor centers cater to varied abilities, ensuring everyone can experience the park's magic.

Know before you go: Rules and Regulations for Responsible Exploration:

Before we leap into adventure, let's speak about duty. Crater Lake's environment is delicate, and it must be respected. Consider this: we are borrowing this natural treasure, and it is our responsibility to keep it in immaculate condition for future generations. Stick to authorized trails, limit your impact, and properly dispose of debris. Remember that you're sharing this environment with amazing wildlife, so keep your distance and appreciate them from afar. By obeying the guidelines, we assure that this Cascades diamond will continue to shine for centuries.

Are you ready to embark on this volcanic adventure with me? Part two promises to reveal the park's hidden beauties, including exhilarating hikes and breathtaking overlooks. Stay tuned, dear travelers; the voyage to Crater Lake National Park is only beginning! We'll drive along the Rim Drive, which offers breathtaking panoramic views, and take hidden trails that lead to cascading waterfalls and secret coves. We'll look into the park's interesting history, unearth the secrets of its fiery past, and maybe even offer some insider tips on where to get the best huckleberry pie (believe me, it's legendary!). So get ready, because Part Two is when the real adventure begins!

CHAPYER 2: TOP ATTRACTIONS

Okay, adventurers, dust off your trekking boots and prepare to have your breath stolen! We're diving right into the heart of Crater Lake National Park, where nature flexes its artistic muscles with jaw-dropping landscapes. Buckle up, because we're about to tour some of the park's most breathtaking sights.

Crater Lake, The Crown Jewel:

Let's start with the main attraction, the reason we're all here: Crater Lake. Consider this: a sapphire diamond so unbelievably blue that it appears to sparkle, nestled amid a volcanic caldera etched by time. Towering evergreens frame the picture, their emerald embrace standing out against the austere grey cliffs that rise in a beautiful arc. This isn't a postcard, folks; it's the genuine deal, and the first look will make you weak in the knees.

But Crater Lake is more than just a gorgeous face; it's an adventure waiting to be discovered. Take the spectacular Rim Drive, a 33-mile volcanic boulevard that follows the caldera's rim. Each twist and bend reveals a fresh breathtaking vista, with Crater Lake shining like a turquoise star in the center. Visit overlooks such as Discovery Point and Watchman's Shelter, where history tells of volcanic devastation and human endurance.

Cleetwood Cove offers a closer glimpse. Take a boat tour and feel the cool spray on your face as you look up at the caldera cliffs, each crack whispering mysteries from the past. Keep an eye out for "The Phantom Ship," a towering rock creation that appears to sail across the lake's surface, like a ghostly sentry from another time.

Feeling adventurous? Lace up your boots and tackle the Wizard Island Hike. This 2-mile hike brings you to the caldera's center, where you may stand on the rim of a dormant cinder cone and look down into the lake. It's a difficult climb, but the panoramic views and sense of accomplishment are worth every drop of sweat.

Beyond the Crown Jewel

Crater Lake may be the star, but its supporting cast is equally impressive. Let's go beyond the rim and find some hidden treasures.

Castle Creek Falls is a flowing symphony tucked within a verdant valley. The 70-foot plunge thunders through a variety of environments, including basalt cliffs and wildflower-filled meadows. Take the Castle Creek Falls Trail, a simple 1.2-mile loop that travels through this lush beauty. Listen to the water's singing, breathe in the fresh mountain air, and let your cares fade away.

Sinnott Memorial Observation Station offers breathtaking panoramic vistas. This historic overlook, positioned on a cliff edge, provides stunning views of the entire caldera, from the lake's glittering surface to the far mountain peaks. It's an ideal position to take in the park's immensity and reflect on the majesty of nature.

Do you crave a secret escape? Follow the twisting road to Plaikni Falls, a hidden beauty buried away in the forest. Sunlight filters through the canopy, lighting the flowing water that tumbles into a moss-covered pool. It's a serene haven, ideal for a quiet period of introspection or a cool swim on a hot summer day.

Unveil the Magic

Crater Lake National Park, however, is more than just a scenic destination; it is an experience that engages all of your senses. Witness the sunrise paint the lake in gold and orange, turning it into a flaming diamond. Hike under a blanket of stars, feeling the vastness of the universe pressing down as you look at the Milky Way reflected in the quiet water. Listen to the wind whisper through the pines, carrying the sounds of volcanic explosions and old stories. Breathe in the fresh mountain air, which will invigorate your soul and leave you feeling linked to something far greater than yourself.

Remember that Crater Lake National Park is a vulnerable ecology. Treat it with respect, leave no trace, and be conscious of the animals that lives here. Let us work together to preserve this natural beauty for future generations.

CHAPTER 3: WILDLIFE VIEWING

Bald Eagles Are Soaring Sentinels of the Sky.

Consider this scenario: you're standing on the lip of Crater Lake, the blue expanse stretched before you like a dream. Suddenly, a piercing and electrifying shriek rings out. You look up and see a majestic bald eagle, its white head sparkling against the azure canvas. As it hovers gently on powerful wings, you are overcome with wonder. You are seeing a live emblem of freedom, a creature that has soared among these heights for millennia.

Bald eagles are more than just gorgeous creatures; they are an essential component of the park's ecosystem.

Watch them scan the lake's surface for fish, their acute gaze unwavering even from above. They make their nests in lofty trees and raise their young with intense protectiveness. Witnessing these majestic birds is a privilege, a reminder of nature's delicate balance and the strength of resilience.

Diverse BirdLife

But the bird display at Crater Lake goes far beyond the famed bald eagle. Listen carefully, and you'll be swept into a symphony of various birdlife, each contributing its own melody to the natural soundtrack.

Black-headed woodpeckers search for hidden insects by tapping a repetitive drumming on worn tree trunks. Their brilliant red tops stand out like embers against the green foliage, bringing a pop of color to the forest's muted tone.

Overhead, the acrobatic Steller's jay flits between branches, its azure plumage a striking contrast to the emerald pine. Its harsh yet lovely call echoes across the woods, lending a whimsical element to the setting.

As nightfall falls, a different chorus takes center stage. Listen for the Western screech owl's mournful call, its strange yet captivating song ringing through the twilight. Look for the elusive Northern flicker, whose golden wings catch the final rays of the setting sun as it flits between treetops.

Loons, the haunting melody of the deep.

The crown jewel of Crater Lake's avian inhabitants lives within its sapphire depths. The eerie call of the common loon rings out across the water, a sound as ancient and evocative as the lake itself. Watch as they effortlessly dive and emerge, their sleek bodies leaving trails of silver ripples behind them. Their somber screams tell stories of resistance and survival, evoking the spirit of the volcanic forces that created this breathtaking terrain.

Encounters in the Wild

Crater Lake National Park is more than simply a visual feast; it is a refuge where nature may be seen in all of her untamed grandeur. Beyond the azure depths and towering pines, a fascinating cast of furry and feathery creatures roam, providing another layer of enchantment to this volcanic haven. Let's go beyond the paved trails and learn about the lives of black-tailed deer and elk, majestic kings of the meadows, and mischievous marmots and pika, alpine masters.

Black-tailed deer, the graceful ghosts of the meadows

Consider this: a gentle breeze stirs the emerald cloak of a meadow, and sunlight dapples the earth. Suddenly, a flash of movement draws your attention: a stately black-tailed deer emerges from the trees, its silky coat glittering in the sun. As it grazes peacefully, you see a creature that is perfectly at ease with its surroundings, a living expression of the park's wild essence.

Black-tailed deer are more than simply lovely dancers in the meadows; they are essential components of the ecology. Watch them munch on wildflowers, their sharp senses alert to any disturbance in the foliage. Observe fawns playing alongside their mothers, learning the delicate balance of survival in this ever-changing environment. Witnessing these creatures is humbling, reminding us of the fragility and beauty of life in the face of nature's majesty.

Elk: Lords of the Open Expanse.

However, the meadows are not solely governed by deer. As you go deeper, listen for the big elk's bugling call, which echoes through the valleys with both power and fragility. These beautiful beasts, with their gorgeous antlers and intimidating stature, elicit respect and awe.

Watch them graze in herds, their movements synced as they migrate across the terrain. Observe calves cuddled with their moms, their lively spirits contrasted with the elders' stoicism. Witnessing these kings of the great expanse reminds us of nature's resilience, its ability to thrive even in the face of changing conditions.

Marmots and Pika: Playful Master of the Alpine

Ascend to the park's highest elevations, where the air thins and the wind whispers stories of perseverance. Amidst the rocky outcrops and vivid wildflowers, you might come across two lively residents: the marmot and the pika.

Marmots, with their rotund proportions and humorous looks, are the alpine jesters. Watch them sunbathe on rocks, whistling warnings to prospective predators and chasing one other in playful tussles. Their colorful personalities bring a sense of comedy to the raw beauty of the high country.

Pika, being smaller and less visible, are masters of concealment. Look carefully among the pebbles for their twitching noses and beady eyes. These tiny bundles of energy run in and out of their burrows, gathering hay for the winter and chirping warnings to their relatives. Witnessing their tenacity and flexibility in this tough environment demonstrates the force of life.

Remember that these creatures are wild and deserve our respect. Observe from a distance, avoid disrupting their habitats, and never try to feed them. By becoming good park stewards, we ensure that future generations can have similar encounters with the unique residents of Crater Lake's wild center.

So lace up your boots, pack your curiosity, and set out on an adventure of exploration. From the graceful deer and majestic elk to the playful marmots and hardworking pika, each encounter offers an opportunity to connect with the natural pulse of this volcanic haven. Allow the creatures of Crater Lake to guide you and behold the raw beauty that emerges before your eyes.

CHAPTER 4: HIKING AND TREKKING TRAILS

Unveiling Crater Lake's Majesty: Hiking Trails for Everyone

Crater Lake National Park is more than simply a scenic beauty; it's a paradise for hikers and trekkers, with routes that wind through emerald forests, skirt the blue lake, and lead to spectacular views. Whether you're an experienced adventurer or a casual walker looking for peaceful strolls, the park has a trail to suit your pace and mood. Let's hike two classic trails: Cleetwood Cove, a modest introduction to the lake's grandeur, and Garfield Peak, a strenuous ascent rewarded with panoramic views.

The Cleetwood Cove Trail offers easy access to stunning beauty.

Imagine you're walking down a lovely route blanketed with pine needles, with dappled sunlight filtering through the emerald canopy. As you walk, the soothing sound of running water fills your ears, bringing you closer to your goal. Suddenly, the spectacular Crater Lake appears before you, its blue depths sparkling in the sun. This, my friends, is the beauty of the Cleetwood Cove Trail, a simple 1-mile loop that provides unrivaled access to the park's crown gem.

This family-friendly walk is suitable for hikers of all ages and abilities. The steady climb leads through a rich forest, with towering pines, vivid wildflowers, and even hidden waterfalls. Keep an eye out for lively squirrels and listen to the tweeting symphony of birds. As you approach the viewpoint, gasp in amazement as the entire lake spreads before you. Watch boats glide across the crystal surface, marvel at the majestic cliffs that cradle the caldera, and bask in the calm of this volcanic wonder.

Cleetwood Cove is more than just a scenic spot; it's also an immersive experience. Take a boat cruise to uncover the lake's mysteries. Descend the slopes to Cleetwood Cove, dip your toes in the crystal-clear water, and feel the spray of a rushing waterfall against your face. This pathway serves as a subtle reminder that often the simplest paths lead to the most satisfying experiences.

Garfield Peak Trail

Are you an adventurer looking for a challenge and breathtaking views? Then lace up your boots and climb Garfield Peak Trail, a 5.2-mile round-trip hike that will put your legs to the test while rewarding you with jaw-dropping views.

This moderate-to-strenuous trail climbs through a variety of habitats, from lush forests to rocky slopes brimming with wildflowers. As you climb switchbacks, the air thins and the sights become more magnificent. Looking back, you can see the blue lake receding in the distance, framed by the caldera's emerald embrace.

The final push to the peak is difficult and exhausting, but the reward is well worth the effort. Reach the summit and be astounded by the 360-degree panorama. Look down into the huge Crater Lake, its blue depths gleaming like a magnificent diamond. Let your gaze wander across the surrounding mountains, their snow-capped summits piercing the azure sky. Feel the wind whisper stories about volcanic explosions and nature's resilience.

Hiking Garfield Peak is more than simply a physical challenge; it's also a journey of personal discovery. As you climb each hill, acknowledge your strength and resilience. As you approach the summit, take in the majesty of the landscape and be humbled by nature's strength. This trail serves as a reminder that the most spectacular views frequently occur after the most difficult climbs.

Remember to respect the park's ecosystem, regardless of which trail you choose. Stay on authorized trails, remove any rubbish, and observe wildlife from a distance. As responsible stewards, we ensure that future generations can enjoy the magic of Crater Lake's hiking routes.

The Echo Canyon Trail

Consider this: you're on a pathway shadowed by towering pines, with sunlight pouring through the canopy onto a path carpeted with volcanic ash. As you descend, the wind delivers whispers from the past, rustling leaves and reverberating over the canyon walls. This, my friends, is the wonder of Echo Canyon Trail, a 1.5-mile round-trip hike that transports you back in time to the spectacular birth of Crater Lake.

This moderate trail is more than just a lovely walk; it's a geological museum created by nature. As you descend, volcanic formations reveal their own stories. Towering cliffs display layers of ash and pumice from Mount Mazama's cataclysmic eruption. Observe the remains of lava flows, their hardened surfaces whispering tales of fire and fury. Imagine the earth trembling, molten rock streaming down slopes, and the formation of the breathtaking Crater Lake.

However, Echo Canyon is more than simply the past; it is also alive in the present. Look for brightly colored wildflowers, listen for bird melodies booming across the canyon, and smell the fresh mountain air that holds whispers of history. Take a moment to stand on the canyon floor with your eyes closed. Listen for echoes from the past, feel the earth quake beneath your feet, and connect with the raw power that fashioned this region.

Hiking the Echo Canyon Trail is more than just exercise; it's a voyage of connection. Connect with the park's volcanic history, witness nature's resilience, and feel the power of the earth beneath your feet. This trail reminds us that even the most dramatic upheavals can result in breathtaking beauty.

Pacific Crest Trail

Are you an adventurer looking to experience epic journeys? Then lace up your boots and conquer a section of the Pacific Crest Trail (PCT) through Crater Lake National Park. This legendary path, which spans 2,650 miles from Mexico to Canada, provides a challenging yet rewarding experience, highlighting the park's diverse landscapes and whispering tales of countless trekkers who came before you.

The PCT within the park provides a variety of options, from short day hikes to multi-day backpacking adventures. Choose a section that corresponds to your experience and time constraints, but be prepared for varied terrain. You'll pass through wildflower-filled meadows, climb challenging switchbacks through towering forests, and crest ridges with panoramic views of the surrounding mountains and, of course, the majestic Crater Lake.

Hiking the PCT is more than just logging miles; it's a journey of self-discovery. Navigating challenging terrain will put your physical and mental limits to the test. Connect with other hikers, sharing stories and camaraderie beneath the vast mountain sky. Feel the freedom of walking a legendary trail, following in the footsteps of countless adventurers who have sought solace and challenge in nature.

Remember that hiking the PCT requires meticulous planning and preparation. Study the terrain, be prepared for bad weather, and leave no trace in this delicate ecosystem. By respecting the trail and its history, you ensure that future generations can enjoy the same sense of freedom and adventure.

CHAPTER 5: PHOTOGRAPHY OPPORTUNITIES

Unveiling the Soul of Crater Lake

Crater Lake National Park is more than just scenery; it's a photographer's paradise, a canvas where nature creates daily masterpieces with every dawn, sunset, and budding wildflower. From the blazing dawn illuminating the caldera cliffs to brilliant meadows brimming with color, each click of your shutter captures a piece of this stunning wilderness. Let's go on a professional exploration of two outstanding photographic opportunities: sunrise and sunset above Crater Lake, and the transient beauty of wildflowers in bloom.

Dawn's Fiery Embrace, Twilight's Farewell Kiss

Imagine yourself sitting on the crater rim, predawn colors tiptoeing over the mountains, promising a scene bathed in gold. The air is filled with expectation as the sun rises, illuminating the area with a flaming palette. This, dear photographer, is the enchantment of shooting a Crater Lake sunrise: a short moment when you see nature's daily masterpiece unfold before your eyes.

As the sun rises, paint the caldera's walls in vivid orange, pink, and purple. Bathe the lake's surface in golden light, catching the mystical dance of mist reflecting the blazing sky. Every click captures a distinct composition, a monument to the fleeting beauty of a new day. Witness Wizard Island emerge from the depths, its silhouette set against the molten canvas above.

Sunset performs a distinct dance, a melancholy farewell before darkness falls. As the sun sets below the horizon, lengthy shadows paint the landscape, illuminating the cliffs in brilliant oranges and reds. Capture the lake's surface converted into a molten mirror that reflects the flaming sky. Watch clouds transform into canvases of ember and gold, with each brushstroke creating a brief masterpiece. Take in the crisp mountain air, enjoy the serenity of the fading light, and express the emotions that this spectacular spectacle elicits.

Remember, patience is a virtue. Arrive early for sunrise and stay past dusk. Scout areas, experiment with angles and compositions, and be respectful of other photographers and park laws. Witnessing and documenting these amazing moments is a privilege that necessitates responsibility and careful observation.

Nature's Kaleidoscope

Crater Lake is more than just a blue gem; it's a beautiful tapestry of wildflowers. From late spring to early October, meadows explode with color, converting the environment into a photographer's dream. Imagine fields of scarlet paintbrush waving in the soft air, exquisite yellow monkeyflowers adorning rocky slopes, and bright lupine painting the hillsides purple and blue.

Each wildflower tells a story of resilience by blooming under adverse conditions and demonstrating the beauty of life in the face of adversity. Get down low and capture the fine features of petals and stamen with macro lenses. Look for insects buzzing from bloom to bloom, which will give life and movement to your compositions.

Remember, these delicate beauties are fleeting. Research blooming seasons and arrange your vacation accordingly. Be aware of your steps, prevent stomping, and leave no trace. By preserving these delicate ecosystems, we ensure that future photographers can capture the same dazzling symphony of color.

Photography at Crater Lake National Park goes beyond taking photographs; it's about capturing the essence of the location. It's about capturing the feelings created by the flaming sunrises, tranquil sunsets, and bright wildflowers in enduring memories. So pack your camera, embrace the spirit of adventure, and let Crater Lake inspire you to create your own photography masterpieces. Remember that the most appealing photos frequently go beyond technical perfection, capturing the essence of a location and sharing it with the world. May your camera capture the secret stories and emotions built into the fabric of Crater Lake National Park.

Creatures of the Night

As sunset paints the caldera rim in amethyst and umber, go on a quiet tour along woodland pathways. The music of insects and rustling leaves builds, creating a beautiful prelude to a nighttime safari. Keep a watch out for the elusive Northern spotted owl, whose piercing golden eyes gleam beneath the moonlight as it hunts softly amid the woods. Listen for the distinctive drumming of a hairy woodpecker, its tireless search for concealed insects reverberating through the silence. Witness bats' elegant dancing in moonlit fields, their echolocation abilities a miracle of adaptability in the dark.

Closer to the water's edge, you may witness river otters play, their sleek bodies shimmering like phantoms as they frolic and hunt in the moonlight. On rare occasions, you may get a glimpse of a coyote, its amber eyes scanning the environment with wary interest. Remember, these species are wild artists who deserve our respect and careful observation. Use red-filtered flashlights to reduce disruption and keep a safe distance, ensuring their continued dance beneath the starlit canvas.

Starry Spectacle

As dusk falls, the universe reveals its stunning creativity above Crater Lake. Look up and be enchanted by the Milky Way, an ethereal band extending across the stardusted sky, exposing myriad cosmic treasures that are undetectable to the naked sight. Consider ancient constellations whispering stories of heroes and mythological monsters, guiding navigators and creating awe across millennia.

Crater Lake's secluded position and low light pollution make it an astronomer's delight. Stargazing apps turn your smartphone into a cosmic map, revealing the mysteries of constellations, planets, and even meteors that streak across the huge canvas. Join a ranger-led astronomy session to dig deeper into the universe, learning about star formation, galactic secrets, and the immensity that exists beyond our world.

Remember, respecting the darkness is essential for preserving this nighttime display. To reduce light pollution, avoid bright lights and use only red-filtered flashlights, enabling your eyes to adjust to the natural darkness. Dress warmly, as temperatures can drop dramatically at night. By embracing darkness and reducing our footprint, we ensure that future generations can feel the same awe as we gaze at the universe, unfurled in all its majesty above Crater Lake.

Wildlife interactions and stargazing trips are more than just experiences; they are invitations. They encourage us to connect with the park's hidden pulse, to observe the delicate balance of nature's nightly tapestry, and to be awed by the majesty and wonder of creation. So, fellow explorers, let us go beyond the familiar and immerse ourselves in the mysteries that emerge beneath the watchful gaze of the moon and the vast expanse of stars. Prepare to be captured by the magic that lies in the shadows of Crater Lake National Park.

CHAPTER 6: ADVENTURE SPORTS

Embrace the Thrill: Adventure Sports at Crater Lake

Crater Lake National Park is more than simply a visual feast; it's an adventure playground, with a plethora of activities that appeal to your sense of discovery and adrenaline. From floating across the lake's mirror-like surface in summer to carving tracks through snowy landscapes in winter, the park has something for every adventurous soul. Let's dive into two amazing experiences, one in the summer warmth and the other in the winter wonderland.

Kayaking and Stand-Up Paddle boarding

Consider this: a beautiful morning breeze whispers through your hair as you glide across the azure expanse of Crater Lake, its depths glittering like a liquid gem. Sunlight dances across the river, while snow-capped peaks outline the horizon. This, my friends, is the magic of kayaking or stand-up paddleboarding on Crater Lake a summer adventure that will transport you to the heart of the park in an unforgettable way.

like you paddle on the crystal surface, feel the cool water beneath your fingertips and the rhythmic movement of your craft like a calm serenade. Allow the silence to envelope you, interrupted only by the occasional cry of a loon or the splash of a playful fish. Examine the towering cliffs that round the caldera, their volcanic history imprinted into their craggy surfaces. Watch Wizard Island rise majestically from the depths, a silent sentinel protecting the lake's mysteries.

Kayaking and stand-up paddle boarding provide unique sensations. Kayaks have a comfortable, enclosed cockpit that is great for calm exploration. Stand-up paddleboards provide a more energetic experience, requiring balance and core strength as you glide across the water. Both alternatives provide access to secluded coves and perspectives that are unavailable by land, immersing you in the lake's unique ecosystem.

Remember that safety is paramount. Before stepping out, attend an orientation session taught by a ranger, carry a life jacket, and check the weather forecast. Respect the lake's vulnerable ecosystem by reducing noise and avoiding disturbing wildlife. As responsible stewards, we ensure that future generations can enjoy the same amazing dance on the sea.

Winter Wonderland

As snow blankets the area, changing Crater Lake into a winter paradise, a new type of adventure begins. Lace up your snowshoes or cross-country skis and set out on a trek through peaceful woodlands and shimmering meadows. Breathe in the cool mountain air, feel the crunch of snow beneath your feet, and watch the park change into a silent world shrouded in white.

For a more thrilling experience, get on a snowmobile and ride approved paths, creating tracks over snow-covered terrain. Feel the wind in your hair as you navigate mild slopes and open meadows, taking in panoramic views of the lake's surrounding snow-capped hills. Remember, responsible snowmobiling is critical. To preserve the tranquility of the winter wonderland, stay on designated pathways, protect wildlife, and reduce noise pollution.

Whether you want a quiet glide through snow-covered trees or an adrenaline-pumping ride through gorgeous surroundings, Crater Lake's winter sports provide amazing experiences. Pack warm clothing, check the weather, and be ready for shifting terrain. By following the park's rules and being environmentally conscious, we ensure that future generations can experience the same winter beauty.

Remember that adventure sports at Crater Lake are about more than simply adrenaline; they are also about connection. Connect with the park's beauty throughout the seasons, push yourself physically and emotionally, and make memories that will last a lifetime. So, embrace the excitement, choose your summer or winter journey, and prepare to be fascinated by the wonders of Crater Lake National Park. Allow the spirit of adventure to lead you as you explore the hidden gems that await you on the water and in the snow.

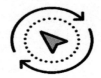

CHAPTER: 7
EDUCATIONAL PROGRAMS

Crater Lake: Where Learning and Adventure Intersect

Crater Lake National Park is more than just a beautiful wonder; it's a portal to discovery, where breathtaking landscapes coexist with enriching educational opportunities. Whether you're a curious child, a lifelong learner, or simply looking for a better understanding, the park has activities that will spark your imagination and quench your hunger for knowledge. Let's look at three different programs that reveal the park's secrets, instill a love of nature in young minds, and provide interactive exhibits that bring its wonders to life.

Ranger-Led Talks and Walks

Consider accompanying a passionate ranger at the spectacular Rim Village, their speech painting vivid images of Mount Mazama's volcanic eruption and Crater Lake's dramatic formation. Witness their contagious enthusiasm as they point out amazing geological features, secret waterfalls, and unusual plant life. This, dear explorer, is the enchantment of ranger-led talks and walks: immersive adventures that reveal the park's secret stories and strengthen your relationship to its beauties.

These programs cater to a wide range of interests and ages. Join a family-friendly stroll and see children's eyes light up as they learn about volcanic rocks, spot lively chipmunks, and discover intriguing information about the lake's unique ecosystem. Immerse yourself in a history-focused hike, walking in the footsteps of early explorers and learning about the park's cultural significance to indigenous tribes. Alternatively, go deeper into geology with a ranger, comprehending the volcanic mysteries carved in the caldera walls and marveling at nature's might.

Remember that rangers are enthusiastic storytellers and knowledgeable guides. Ask questions, participate actively, and welcome the opportunity to benefit from their experience. Supporting these initiatives helps the park's conservation efforts and ensures that future generations can enjoy the same enjoyable experiences.

Junior Ranger Activities

Are you hearing delighted squeals ringing across the park? Look for children proudly sporting Junior Ranger badges, which demonstrate their involvement in engaging activities that foster a love of wildlife and environmental care. Crater Lake's Junior Ranger program is more than

simply a good time; it's also an educational adventure that encourages curiosity and responsibility.

Children go on interactive expeditions, guided by activity books loaded with riddles, scavenger hunts, and challenges that take them across various park environments. Imagine them sketching wildflowers, measuring tree heights, and learning about animal adaptations, all while earning badges and developing a greater respect for the park's delicate environmental balance.

These activities are not just for children; they are ideal for families to bond via shared learning opportunities. Parents can experience their own childhood wonders while leading their children on a journey of exploration. Remember that instilling a love of nature in young minds is critical to its preservation, and Crater Lake's Junior Ranger program plays an important role in this effort.

Crater Lake Discovery

As you approach the Crater Lake Discovery Center, its modern architecture fits in with the surrounding scenery, enticing you to go on an interactive journey through the park's attractions. Step inside and you'll be met by captivating exhibits that use technology, interactive displays, and hands-on activities to bring the park's history, geology, and ecosystem alive.

Imagine looking down into the lake's depths with a high-resolution underwater camera, observing the rare living forms that flourish in its crystal-clear waters. Explore interactive models depicting Mount Mazama's dramatic birth and the development of the caldera. Watch engaging films that describe the lake's cultural significance to local populations.

Whether you are a seasoned park enthusiast or a first-time visitor, the Discovery Center has something for everyone. Learn about the park's diverse fauna through educational displays and interactive games. Immerse yourself in the fascinating story of its volcanic origins with touch-screen exhibits and instructional videos. Remember, this is more than simply a museum; it is a portal to a better understanding and enjoyment of the park's beauties.

More than just programs:

Crater Lake's educational initiatives extend beyond conventional formats. Every trek, boat excursion, and ranger contact provides a unique learning experience. Keep an eye out for interpretive signs throughout the park that provide information about the flora, animals, and geological wonders around you. Ask questions, participate in conversations with other visitors and park workers, and let your curiosity to guide your tour.

Embrace the park's natural classroom. Listen to the wind whispering through the pines, admire the fine features of a wildflower, and feel the refreshing spray of a falling waterfall. These sensory experiences, together with the knowledge gained from programs and self-exploration, result in a comprehensive learning experience that will stay with you long after you leave.

Remember, Crater Lake is more than simply a gorgeous spot; it's a living laboratory waiting to be discovered. With its numerous educational activities and experiential learning possibilities, the park sparks interest in

CHAPTER 8: MY SUGGESTED ADDITIONS

A professional exploration of Crater Lake National Park's multifaceted heart.

Beyond its spectacular beauty, Crater Lake National Park provides a tapestry of engaging experiences that dive into its volcanic past, cultural legacy, and artistic inspiration. Beyond the azure depths and towering pines is a plethora of programs and activities designed to pique your interest and deepen your awareness of this extraordinary area. Allow us to embark on a professional adventure, going beyond the typical tourist trail and into the heart of the park's diverse essence.

Geology and Volcanology Tours

Imagine yourself standing on the brink of Crater Lake, its sapphire depths whispering stories from a fiery past. Join a renowned geologist for a guided tour that turns the countryside into a living classroom. The traces of Mount Mazama's dramatic eruption are carved into the towering rocks. Feel the heat from volcanic vents and touch the silky obsidian made from molten lava. These tours are more than just recitations of facts; they are immersive experiences that reveal the complicated story of the park's origin, the interaction of magma, ash, and ice that formed the lake, and the ongoing geological processes that continue to sculpt this dynamic landscape. Engage your senses, ask questions, and develop a deep respect for the Earth's strong forces and the park's extraordinary evolution.

Cultural and Tribal History Programs

As you stand in awe of the lake's immensity, examine the diverse cultural heritage woven into its fabric. Participate in a program guided by local indigenous groups and go on a trip through time to discover the strong bond between these people and the land. Hear stories passed down through generations about creation, spiritual beliefs, and ecological activities that align with the rhythm of the earth. Witness traditional dances and songs, which are more than just performances; they are living testaments to indigenous peoples' long-standing bond with this valued territory. These programs are more than just informative; they promote connections and understanding, encouraging respectful dialogue and collaboration to preserve the park's distinct character and the cultural history that nourishes it.

Art and Photography Workshops

Imagine the sunrise lighting up the sky, its brilliant hues reflected on the lake's surface. Instead of taking a hasty photo, imagine yourself under the tutelage of an experienced artist, transforming the emotions and beauty around you into a timeless masterpiece. This is the essence of Crater Lake's painting and photography workshops: translating observation into artistic expression for all skill levels. Learn from specialists about composition, lighting, and capturing the park's essence through various mediums. Whether you use a paintbrush, a camera lens, or a sculptor's chisel, the park's breathtaking vistas and rich flora and animals provide limitless inspiration. Remember, these workshops are about more than just making art; they are about developing a stronger connection with the park. Slowing down, analyzing details, and putting your feelings onto art or film gives you a new appreciation for the park's intricate beauty and ability to inspire. Share your creations with others, starting conversations and building a sense of community around the park's artistic expressions.

Beyond Ordinary: A Transformative Journey Awaits

Crater Lake National Park provides more than simply breathtaking views; it invites you to go deeper, to discover its fiery history, colorful cultural heritage, and artistic inspiration. Participating in these unique events transforms you into more than just a visitor; you become a storyteller, steward, and artist, leaving your own imprint on the park's ever-changing tale. So bundle your curiosity, choose your adventure, and embark on a professional journey that goes beyond the usual. Allow the geologists to lead you through the Earth's fiery symphony, while the cultural programs connect you to the region's rich legacy and the art classes encourage you to portray the park's beauty in your own unique way. Remember that Crater Lake is more than simply a destination; it is an experience that awaits your participation, curiosity, and willingness to venture beyond the surface.

CHAPTER 9: ACTIVITIES FOR EVERY TRAVELER

Unveiling the Multifaceted Jewel: Customizing Your Crater Lake Experience

Beyond its breathtaking landscape, Crater Lake National Park provides a diversity of experiences meant to pique varied interests and leave lasting impressions. Whether you're a nature lover looking for quiet moments, a seasoned hiker looking for difficult ascents, or an adrenaline-fueled adventurer looking for thrilling activities, the park has a trail for you. Lace up your boots, grab your binoculars, or get your camera ready for a perfectly planned adventure at Crater Lake, where nature's beauties unveil with each step you take.

For nature enthusiasts

Crater Lake provides a sanctuary for people seeking peaceful contemplation, immersing them in nature's symphony. Embrace quiet mornings in hidden meadows, where songbirds chirp and leaves rustle. Train your binoculars on secretive creatures such as the Northern spotted owl, which has penetrating golden eyes and surveys its territory under the starry sky.

Alternatively, watch river otters play at the water's edge, their sleek bodies shimmering under the watchful gaze of the stars. Remember that these species are wild artists who need to be observed with respect and disturbed as little as possible. By using red-filtered flashlights and at a safe distance, you become a responsible steward, ensuring that future generations can enjoy the same peaceful communion with nature's beauties.

For the Determined Hiker

Crater Lake provides a landscape carved by volcanic fury for those seeking tough ascents, with trails that challenge your resilience while rewarding you with breathtaking panoramas. Ascend Garfield Peak, a 5.2-mile round-trip hike, and feel the rush of completing each switchback, your gaze rewarded by the ever-shrinking sapphire diamond hidden beneath the caldera.

For a more modest challenge, try the Cleetwood Cove Trail, a gentle beginning that reveals stunning lake views with each step. Remember that safety is paramount. Research trail conditions, be prepared for changeable weather, and show respect to other hikers by observing etiquette and reducing noise pollution. By following responsible practices, you help to preserve these famous pathways for future generations of summit seekers.

For the Thrill Seeking Adventurer

Crater Lake is a wonderland for adrenaline junkies, offering thrilling aquatic and winter activities. Glide over the lake's mirror-like surface on a kayak or stand-up paddleboard, feeling the cool water beneath your fingertips and the lovely breeze brushing against your hair. Explore secluded coves that are unreachable by land and become immersed in the lake's unique nature.

In the winter, put on your snowshoes or cross-country skis and cut paths through immaculate powder, surrounded by snow-capped peaks and the quiet calm of the winter wonderland. Remember, responsible fun is essential. Wear life jackets and keep an eye on the weather whether kayaking or paddleboarding. In the winter, stay on authorized pathways and respect wildlife. By putting safety first and limiting environmental effect, you ensure that future adventurers can have the same thrilling interactions with our unique area.

Aside from the scheduled events, keep in mind that the most meaningful experiences frequently occur naturally. Take a moment to simply be present, take in the cool mountain air, and allow the whispering of the forest, the calls of birds, and the grandeur of the lake to work their magic on your heart and soul. Crater Lake is more than simply a tourist destination; it's a place to feel, connect, and discover your inner explorer. So, begin on your journey, accept the unknown, and let the park's story weave itself into your own.

For the history buff

For those who enjoy the past, Crater Lake captivates the imagination with historic lodges full of legends and volcanic scenery whispering tales of fiery creation. Step back in time at the historic Crater Lake Lodge, whose rustic appeal recalls the early days of tourism and provides fascinating glimpses into the park's growth. Explore the geology displays and marvel at artifacts depicting Mount Mazama's eruption and the lake's dramatic creation. Join ranger-led presentations where passionate storytellers transport you back to the time of indigenous people and early explorers who first witnessed this natural wonder. Remember that respect and preservation are vital. Treat these historic treasures with care, recognizing their significance and ensuring that future generations can hear their intriguing stories.

For Relaxation and Rejuvenation

Crater Lake offers a peaceful sanctuary for individuals looking to reconnect with nature and recharge their soul. Take a picturesque drive along Rim Drive, meandering among tall trees and revealing breathtaking views of the sapphire lake below. Pause at designated views, breathe in the fresh mountain air, and let the scenery wash over you, removing your worries and restoring inner serenity. Relax by the lake's shore, spreading out a picnic blanket and enjoying tasty delicacies while the gentle lapping of waves produces a soothing symphony. As twilight colors the sky, sleep beneath a blanket of stars and watch the celestial show unfold above the magnificent caldera. Remember, appropriate enjoyment is essential. Reduce noise pollution, respect designated locations, and leave no trace of your presence to ensure the serenity is preserved for future seekers of solace.

For families

For families wishing to create memories and instill a love of nature, Crater Lake provides a playground of entertaining activities and instructive adventures. Take the Cleetwood Cove Trail, a moderate trail ideal for tiny legs that leads to breathtaking lake views and secret waterfalls. Pack Junior Ranger booklets to turn the trek into an interactive quest in which children may learn about park ecosystems and earn badges while having fun. Ranger-led programs for young minds feature compelling storytelling that brings park history and animals to life through interactive activities and games.

Remember that instilling a connection with nature in children is critical for its preservation. By choosing ethical activities and leaving no trace, you ensure that future generations can have similar enriching experiences with their family.

Aside from these specialized experiences, keep in mind that the most fascinating discoveries at Crater Lake frequently occur naturally. Spend some time wandering down hidden trails, admiring the brilliant wildflowers, and listening to the wind whispering through the pines. Allow the tranquility of the lake, the majesty of the volcanic terrain, and the whispers of history to work their magic on your voyage. Crater Lake is more than simply a destination; it's an invitation to explore, learn, and make lifelong memories in the midst of nature's masterpiece. So, embark on your unique voyage, embrace the spirit of exploration, and let Crater Lake reveal its wonders to you.

CHAPTER 10: ITINERARIES FOR DIFFERENT VISITS

Unveiling Crater Lake's Treasures: Customized Itineraries for Every Traveler

Crater Lake National Park, with its breathtaking blue depths and spectacular caldera, entices visitors of various backgrounds and lengths. Whether you're a quick explorer looking for a taste of the park's charms or a seasoned adventurer looking for a deeper immersion, the park has itineraries designed to reveal its distinctive riches. So, pack your curiosity, tie on your walking shoes, and prepare to be fascinated by the many experiences that crater Lake offers:

1-Day Exploration

Hitting the Highlights for Time-Constrained Travelers

Morning: Start your day at Rim Village, where brilliant hues ignite the caldera cliffs and paint the lake's surface in golden magnificence. Capture this spectacular spectacle with your camera before heading out on the Cleetwood Cove Trail, a gentle 1.1-mile loop that leads to hypnotic lake vistas and access to stunning Annie Spring. Return to Rim Village for a quick breakfast while admiring the spectacular scenery.

Midday: Join a ranger-led discussion at the Crater Lake Discovery Center about the park's interesting volcanic history and diverse ecology. Alternatively, take a boat cruise on the lake to see its crystal-clear depths and distinct environment from a different angle. Pack a picnic lunch to enjoy by the lake, taking in the tranquility and gorgeous scenery.

Afternoon: Hike the Castle Point Trail, a moderate 2.2-mile circle with panoramic views of the surrounding countryside and unrivaled views of Wizard Island. If you have time, examine the displays inside the Rim Visitor Center to learn more about the park's cultural significance and geological marvel. Finish your day with dinner at Crater Lake Lodge, where you can enjoy wonderful food while taking in the historic atmosphere.

Weekend Getaway

Immerse yourself in the Park's Wonders

Day 1: Begin your tour at Rim Village, where you may experience a breathtaking sunrise and photograph its stunning colors. Embark on the tough but rewarding Garfield Peak Trail, a 5.2-mile roundtrip excursion that ends with stunning panoramic views of the entire caldera. Enjoy a picnic lunch on the peak, enjoying a sense of satisfaction as you bask in the fruits of your labor.

Afternoon: Spend the rest of the day exploring the park's numerous activities. Kayak or stand-up paddleboard through the lake's pristine waters to gain a new perspective on its distinct environment. Join a ranger-led session to learn more about the park's cultural value and the history of indigenous cultures that have revered this place for millennia.

Evening: Attend an astronomy presentation under the starry sky, taking in the cosmic spectacle unfolding over the spectacular caldera. Savor a superb meal at Crater Lake Lodge while reminiscing on the day's adventures in the historic setting.

Day 2: Begin your day with a calm sunrise meditation by the lake, soaking up the serenity and connecting with the natural beauty around you. Hike the hard but rewarding Kings Castle Trail, a 4.4-mile loop with diverse scenery and stunning views of the lake and surrounding peaks.

Afternoon: Relax by the lake and enjoy a picturesque picnic surrounded by breathtaking views. Participate in a Junior Ranger session taught by a ranger, where your children will engage in interactive activities that will instill a love of wildlife and a respect for the park's treasures. Conclude your weekend with a leisurely drive down Rim Drive, taking in the stunning surroundings and catching last glimpses of the park's charm before you leave.

Remember, these are simply starting points. Customize these itineraries to meet your interests, fitness level, and time constraints. Research trails and activities before of time, arrange lodging accordingly, and prioritize responsible practices to ensure the park's beauty is preserved for future years.

Beyond these proposed itineraries, the true enchantment of Crater Lake resides in deviating from the intended course. Follow a hidden trail, engage in a compelling conversation with a ranger, or simply relax by the lake and let nature's whispers guide your journey. Allow yourself to be attracted by the unexpected, since these unforeseen events frequently leave the strongest impressions.

So, begin on your personal journey, embrace the spirit of adventure, and let Crater Lake reveal its hidden riches to you. Remember that it is more than just a destination; it is an invitation to discover, connect, and make memories that will last a lifetime.

CHAPTER 11: ESSENTIAL INFORMATION

Crater Lake National Park's breathtaking beauty and different experiences make for an amazing journey. Regardless of your budget, preferred lodgings, or exploration style, careful planning may ensure a seamless and enjoyable journey. This guide will provide you with the necessary information to unlock the park's charm responsibly and sustainably.

Lodging & Dining

Customizing Your Comfort and Culinary Experience

In-park Options:

Crater Lake Lodge: A historic structure with breathtaking lake views, pleasant rooms, a renowned restaurant, and a gift shop. Ideal for people who value both grandeur and convenience.

Mazama Village Campground: This campground, located near the Visitor Center, offers basic amenities for tent and RV camping in a natural setting. Ideal for budget-conscious travellers.

Nearby Options

Munson Lodge: This rustic sanctuary, located just outside the park entry, provides lovely cottages, wonderful meals, and a family-friendly ambiance. Ideal for people looking for a relaxing hideaway with convenient access to the park.

Munson and Union Creek are attractive villages with a variety of hotels, cabins, and vacation rentals, as well as restaurants, stores, and gas stations. Ideal for experiencing local character while remaining close to diverse sites of interest.

Budget-conscious choices:

Camping: Many campgrounds outside the park offer low-cost options, including the East Rim and Manzanita Lake Campgrounds. Remember to get permits in advance.

Picnics: Pack excellent dinners and snacks to eat at gorgeous vistas or by the lake, allowing you to enjoy the park's splendor while saving money.

Dining:

Crater Lake Lodge Restaurant: This establishment serves breakfast, lunch, and dinner with beautiful lake views, catering to a wide range of tastes.

Rim Village restaurant: This restaurant serves quick and convenient meals within the park, making it ideal for visitors seeking uncomplicated fare.

Munson Lodge Restaurant: Enjoy delicious breakfasts, dinners, and breathtaking mountain vistas at our family-friendly restaurant.

Local Restaurants: Visit adjacent towns for a distinct dining experience, which can range from casual cafés to gourmet dining venues.

Remember to book lodgings well in advance, especially during high season. When choose where to stay, keep your budget, desired level of comfort, and access preferences in mind.

Camping and backpacking

Obtaining Permits and Regulations:

Secure camping permits ahead of time by visiting the park's website or Visitor Center.

Backpacking permits are required for overnight stays outside of authorized campgrounds.

To reduce environmental damage, follow all fire regulations and camp only in specified areas.

Responsible practices

Use Leave No Trace principles to reduce impact by packing out all rubbish, respecting wildlife, and avoiding disturbing plants.

Prepare for uncertain weather by carrying proper gear and wearing in layers.

To avoid attracting wildlife, store food securely.

Follow campfire restrictions and extinguish any fires before leaving.

Choose trails appropriate for your fitness level and experience.

By following these responsible behaviors, you help to preserve Crater Lake's mystique and ensure that future generations can enjoy its unspoiled beauty.

Additional considerations:

Accessibility: The park has accessible overlooks, paths, and services for those with impairments.

Pet Policies: Leashed pets are permitted on paved roads and specified trails, but cleanup must be done responsibly.

Cell service is limited throughout the park. Make the required arrangements in advance, and consider downloading offline maps or using applications.

Embrace the adventure.

Crater Lake National Park offers more than just stunning scenery; it invites you to explore, interact with nature, and make lasting experiences. With this vital book, you'll be able to plan your own trip, whether it's taking on difficult hikes, canoeing across the beautiful lake, or simply relaxing in the winter beauty. Remember that prudent planning enhances your enjoyment while preserving the park's assets for future generations.

So pack your curiosity, lace up your boots, and prepare to be fascinated by the beauty of Crater Lake National Park.

Transportation

Personal Vehicle: The most adaptable option, allowing you to explore at your own leisure and reach remote locations. Remember that parking at popular sites can be restricted, so plan appropriately.

Park Shuttle: During high season, a free shuttle runs throughout Rim Village, connecting main attractions and relieving parking difficulties.

Bicycles: Take a leisurely ride along designated pathways while enjoying the fresh air and gorgeous views. Remember that bike helmets are necessary.

Nearby towns include Medford-Rogue Valley International Airport, which is about 80 miles from the park entrance. Rental cars are available.

Klamath Falls Airport: A smaller airport located 90 miles from the park that also provides rental vehicle services.

There are limited public transit options in the area. Using ride-sharing services or planning planned tours may be more convenient options.

Remember to check for road closures and winter weather conditions before your visit. Always adhere to park traffic regulations and parking limitations.

Visitor Centers & Park Headquarters

Rim Visitor Center: Located within Rim Village, this facility provides park maps, displays, ranger programs, and a bookstore. Perfect for basic orientation and acquiring permits.

Steel Visitor Center: Open year-round, this center near the South Entrance offers information, displays, and restrooms.

Park Headquarters: Located outside the park near Munson Valley, this administrative office provides detailed information and backcountry permits.

Pro Tip: Use visitor centers as a hub for arranging your adventure, getting recommendations from park rangers, and receiving important safety information.

Additional resources: deepening your discovery. Beyond The Surface

National Park Service Website: The official park website *https://www.nps.gov/crla/*

contains detailed information about park regulations, current conditions, future events, and educational materials.

Crater Lake Institute: This non-profit organization *https://www.craterlakeinstitute.com/*

provides educational programs, guided walks, and cultural activities to help you comprehend the park's various facets.

Beyond the Guide: The most interesting discoveries at Crater Lake frequently occur naturally. Engage in ranger talks, strike up conversations with other explorers, and let the whispers of the forest and the grandeur of the lake guide your path. By following appropriate practices and utilizing these tools, you can maximize the value of your Crater Lake trip.

So, pack your spirit of adventure, choose your course, and prepare to be captivated by the delights that lie ahead. Remember that Crater Lake is more than simply a destination; it's an invitation to discover, connect, and weave your own remarkable tale into the tapestry of this natural wonder.

CHAPTER 12: BEYOND THE PARK

Unveiling the Enchantment and Exploring Beyond Crater Lake's borders

Crater Lake National Park is filled with enthralling wonder, yet its allure stretches far beyond the crater rim. This final part takes you outside the park's boundaries, into the region's rich tapestry of lovely villages, hidden jewels, and sustainable travel practices.

Exploring Nearby Towns and Attractions

Munson and Union Creek: These small communities adjoining the park welcome visitors with snug cabins, local cafes, and businesses promoting regional goods. Immerse yourself in the local culture while eating excellent food and perusing unique souvenirs.

Fort Klamath is a historic military station where visitors can explore renovated structures and learn about the region's rich history. Immerse yourself in displays that document Native American history and early settler contacts.

Diamond Lake and Toketee Lake: Take picturesque drives around these beautiful lakes, stopping for tranquil hikes through old forests or participating in water activities such as kayaking and paddleboarding. Enjoy the tranquility of these hidden retreats.

Lava Beds National Monument: Discover the exotic splendor of volcanic landscapes by visiting lava caverns, cinder cones, and massive rock formations. To learn about this flaming past, take interpretive hikes or participate in ranger-led programs.

Day Trips to Bend, Oregon

Bend, located 90 minutes from Crater Lake, combines outdoor activity with urban flair. Explore art galleries filled with local talent, eat locally sourced specialties at renowned restaurants, and browse unusual boutiques along bustling streets.

Hike picturesque paths such as Misery Ridge and Paulina Peak, which provide panoramic views and different terrains. Kayak down the Deschutes River, immersing yourself in the soothing embrace of the water while seeing the plentiful animals.

Indulge in craft beers at Bend's renowned breweries, and experience the city's thriving brewing sector. Immerse yourself in the colorful ambiance and try the unique flavors.

Visit the High Desert Museum, which explores the region's natural history, cultures, and artistic traditions. Engage with interactive exhibits to obtain a better grasp of the landscape you're experiencing.

Sustainable travel practices

Reduce, reuse, and recycle: Reduce waste by bringing reusable water bottles, food containers, and shopping bags. Use the recycling facilities supplied by the park and adjacent municipalities.

Respect wildlife and vegetation. To reduce environmental disturbance, keep a safe distance from wildlife, do not feed them, and stick to authorized pathways.

Minimize water consumption by using park-provided water stations and practicing appropriate water use while camping or trekking.

Leave no trace: Dispose of all waste, including ostensibly biodegradable objects such as cigarette butts and fruit peels. To reduce the impact of campfires, follow laws and properly extinguish them.

Choose locally owned restaurants, stores, and hotels to help the region's economy and preserve its unique flavor.

Adopting these behaviors ensures that future generations can enjoy the same breathtaking beauty and cultural diversity that captured you. Leave only footprints of admiration and respect as a custodian of this lovely place.

Embrace the Unforeseen: The most enriching discoveries are often spontaneous. Strike up talks with locals, take picturesque detours, and let the spirit of adventure drive you. Relax with live music under a starry sky in Bend, discover secret waterfalls along winding roads, or simply enjoy the tranquility of a peaceful sunset beside a neighboring lake. Crater Lake is only the beginning; embrace the region's rich tapestry and weave your own remarkable story into it.

So, go beyond the rim, explore with an open heart, and make a constructive impression on the areas that speak to your spirit. Remember that responsible travel is more than just reducing your carbon footprint; it is also about taking an active role in protecting the treasures that enhance our lives.

This last chapter brings the entire guide to a close, providing you with the knowledge and inspiration you need to plan a personalized and sustainable experience that goes beyond Crater Lake National Park's limits. May your trip be full of discoveries, respect, and unforgettable memories.

APPENDIX

While I cannot put specific park maps, trail guides, or contact information here, I can point you to important resources that are easily accessible online:

The official Crater Lake National Park website https://www.nps.gov/crla/

includes downloadable maps, detailed trail guides, and important visitor information.

Park Brochures and Maps: Physical copies of brochures, maps, and wildlife identification guides can be obtained in the Crater Lake Lodge gift store or any park visitor center. Remember to support these vital park facilities throughout your visit.

Third-Party Resources: Reputable outdoor goods and recreation websites frequently include downloadable park maps and trail guides. Before using any information, ensure that it is accurate and up to date.

Wildlife Identification:

National Park Service Field Guides: The National Park Service provides a variety of field guides tailored to Crater Lake and the surrounding area. Consider buying one online or from a park bookshop for thorough information and illustrations of local fauna.

Mobile Apps: Look into downloaded apps like iNaturalist or Seek, which help you identify plants and animals based on photos or audio recordings. Remember to appreciate wildlife by practicing responsible observation and keeping a safe distance.

Local Weather Information:

The National Weather Service website provides hourly and extended forecasts for the Crater Lake area.

Park Website and Social Media: Keep up to date on current weather conditions, road closures, and potential hazards by visiting the Crater Lake National Park website and following its social media outlets.

Emergency Contact Information:

Park Rangers: For immediate assistance in the park, dial 911 or call (541) 594-3000.

Klamath County Sheriff's Office: For emergencies outside the park, call (541) 883-5130.

National Park Service Emergency Hotline: For national park help, call 888-647-7275.

Remember that your safety and responsible actions are paramount. Familiarize oneself with park rules, be prepared for changing weather, and respect wildlife and the environment. By doing so, you help to preserve the magic of Crater Lake for future generations.

THANK YOU PAGE

Thank you for joining me on this journey through Crater Lake National Park! Your curiosity and time are greatly appreciated. If you enjoyed the book or have thoughts to share, I'd love to hear from you. Feel free to leave your feedback in the comment section. Safe travels and happy reading!

Printed in Great Britain
by Amazon